Badiru's Equation of Student Success

Intelligence, Common Sense, and Self-Discipline

Books in the ABICS Publications Series

Badiru, Deji, **Badiru's Equation of Success: Intelligence, Common Sense, and Self-discipline**, iUniverse, Bloomington, Indiana, USA, 2013

Badiru, Iswat and Deji Badiru, *Isi Cookbook: Collection of Easy Nigerian Recipes*, iUniverse, Bloomington, Indiana, USA, 2013

Badiru, Deji and Iswat Badiru, *Physics in the Nigerian Kitchen: The Science, the Art, and the Recipes*, iUniverse, Bloomington, Indiana, USA, 2013.

Badiru, Deji, *Physics of Soccer: Using Math and Science to Improve Your Game*, iUniverse, Bloomington, Indiana, USA, 2010.

Badiru, Deji, *Getting things done through project management*, iUniverse, Bloomington, Indiana, USA, 2009.

ABICS Publications

A Division of
AB International Consulting Services (ABICS)

www.ABICSPublications.com

Books for home, work, and leisure

Badiru's Equation of Student Success

Intelligence, Common Sense, and Self-Discipline

Deji Badiru

iUniverse, Inc.
Bloomington

Badiru's Equation of Student Success
Intelligence, Common Sense, and Self-Discipline

iUniverse books may be ordered through booksellers or by contacting:

iUniverse
1663 Liberty Drive
Bloomington, IN 47403
www.iuniverse.com
1-800-Authors (1-800-288-4677)

ISBN: 978-1-4759-8021-9 (sc)
ISBN: 978-1-4759-8022-6 (e)

Printed in the United States of America

iUniverse rev. date: 03/01/2013

Dedication

To my wife, Iswat, through whom the art of
self-discipline is fully manifested.

Acknowledgments

I acknowledge and thank all my former students at Tennessee Tech University, the University of Central Florida, the University of Oklahoma, the University of Tennessee, and the Air Force Institute of Technology. They demonstrated exceptional self-discipline in each and every one of my classes so that our instructional goals could be accomplished together as an intellectual team.

Deji Badiru
3 February 2013

Preface

This book presents a compilation of the author's techniques used over a 30-year teaching career for mentoring, encouraging, and chastising (when needed) his students to elicit better performance from each student. The techniques often involve a combination of "tender loving care," when deserved, and stern "hard-nosed" approach (when warranted). The book presents the author's famous "equation of success," the dreaded "recipe for an F," and general guide for time management. The book is purposely designed to be brief and to the point to encourage readers' read-through. Although the book focuses on university education, the guidance is equally applicable to high school students as well. Badiru's equation of success is a guide for encouragement and mentorship rather than a book of indictment.

Table of Contents

Chapter 1

The College Education Process

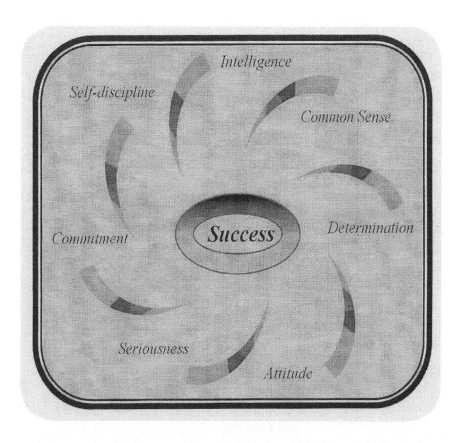

"When curiosity is established, the urge to learn develops."
    –   Deji Badiru

When Albert Einstein was still a lecturing professor, one of his students came to him and said:
"The questions of this year's exam are the same as last year's!"
"True," Einstein responded, "but this year all the answers are different."

"You cannot teach a man anything; you can only help him discover it in himself."
    –   Galileo

T here is a lot that is involved in delivering and acquiring education at the college level. It is a potpourri of systems and subsystems. All of these must be in good consonance in order to achieve the intended results and success. The approach of this book is to look at a few specific factors that revolve around the success of a college student. Of particular interest is the interplay between innate intelligence, common sense, and self-discipline. Readers and parents may expand the basic presentations to fit their specific situations and educational scenarios.

This book presents a personal management approach to student success. The proven techniques of formal project management are recommended as effective approaches to achieving the objectives of student success. The book is deliberately written in an informal list-oriented style to facilitate ease of reference. The book is intended to assist both students and instructors in the pursuit of the activities necessary for satisfactory completion of college education. The pursuit of college education is an individual matter, buttressed by the support of the family and the academic institution. It is the responsibility of the student to take the appropriate action at the appropriate time.

The moral of the introductory proclamation quotes at the beginning of this chapter is that students must be ready, adaptive, and perceptive in the educational process. They must embrace situational awareness to take advantage of the opportunities that present themselves. This is what paves the way for sustainable academic success. College education is very complex and demanding. Surviving in this highly stressful environment takes a good mixture of intelligence, common sense, self-discipline, and good personal organization. There are academic requirements to coping with college education and there are also personal management requirements. While much has been said and written about academic requirements, very little guidelines are available for being a personal factor in the education process itself. Being a personal factor requires good personal management attributes of the student to play his or her own roles and responsibilities in the education process. To be a complete educated person requires efforts outside of the conventional educational process. It should be recalled that many of the learned professionals, engineers, doctors, artists, and theologians of centuries ago were self-taught. Abraham Lincoln, a noted lawyer, was entirely self-taught. His achievements, leading to being elected the 16th president of the United States, confirmed a high level of self-discipline and common sense in addition to his native intelligence.

Peculiarities of College Education

While attempting to make the most out of student-teacher interactions, I have found that many students lack the basic elements that facilitate the education process. Unfortunately, there are very few formal avenues for teaching students how to properly manage their academic programs. College education requires students with professional maturity, who are motivated and committed to learning. They must play an active role in their education and understand the value of learning as a life-long professional goal. They must also have a clear perception of their career and educational objectives. Each student must approach the academic challenge with dedication and utmost commitment. As an educator, I am particularly a stickler for eliciting personal responsibility from students. Students are expected to demonstrate a whole-person capability covering a variety of skills and personal attributes. Some of these include the following:

- Time consciousness
- Interpersonal etiquette
- Taking personal responsibility

- Effective communication
- Adequate preparation for class
- Good study habits
- Compliance with institutional requirements
- Conformance with social norms and standards
- Contingency planning with respect to "Murphy's Law"
- Learning to allow sufficient lead time between consecutive activities
- Planning, scheduling, and controlling study-related activities
- Managing independent assignments
- Familiarization with university resources, such as libraries, labs, etc.
- Positive interactions with other students

Most students entering college are assumed to already have a good level of academic preparation. Where they need help is with being organized and managing themselves well. Essential characteristics for success with college education include the following:

- Intelligence
- Ingenuity
- Creativity
- Self organization and management
  - ➢ Organize, organize, organize, and organize again
- Knowing where everything is kept to minimize non-value-adding search times

Knowledge and smartness alone are not enough to succeed with college education. College students must have the skills necessary to apply knowledge and the attitude required to become responsible and ethical professionals. Skills such as those required for effective learning, problem solving, and communication cannot be learned in the traditional lecture format. Students must exhibit the motivation, self-discipline, and dedication for doing more outside class to enhance classroom success.

Securing the future through education

Education is the most stable investment in securing a satisfying future. A needs-based assessment of personal drive is essential to pursuing college education. Self-motivation and commitment will enhance the ability to meet personal needs. The student's personal social needs should be taken into account in the education process. **Maslow's "Hierarchy of Needs"** suggests the following categories as possible drivers for adapting to the hierarchical demands of college education:

Physiological Needs: The needs for the basic things of life; such as food, water, housing, and clothing. This is the level where access to money is most critical.

Safety Needs: The needs for security, stability, and freedom from threat of physical harm. The fear of adverse environmental impact may inhibit project efforts.

Social Needs: The needs for social approval, friends, love, affection, and association. For example, public service projects may bring about better economic outlook that may enable individuals to be in a better position to meet their social needs.

Esteem Needs: The needs for accomplishment, respect, recognition, attention, and appreciation. These needs are important not only at the individual level, but also at the national level.

Self-actualization Needs: These are the needs for self-fulfillment and self-improvement. They also involve the availability of opportunity to grow professionally. Improvement projects on the job may lead to self-actualization opportunities for individuals to assert themselves socially and economically. Job achievement and professional recognition are two of the most important factors that lead to employee satisfaction and better motivation. The figure below summarizes the essentials of Maslow's hierarchy of needs. College education is a sustainable platform for meeting the needs of each individual.

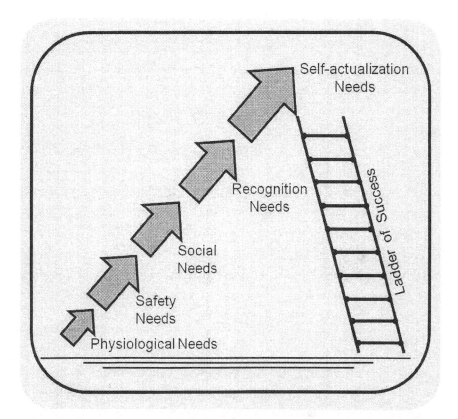

Hierarchical motivation implies that the particular motivation technique utilized for a given person should depend on where the person stands in the hierarchy of needs listed above. For example, the needs for esteem take precedence over the physiological needs when the latter are relatively well satisfied. Money, for example, cannot be expected to be a very successful motivational factor for an individual who is already on the fourth level of the hierarchy of needs.

Is College Education Worth It?

You bet your dollar. Yes, college education is more than worth it. Because of the economic challenges starting in the mid-2000s, the question of whether college education is worth it or not has been coming up more and more. That the question would even come up at all is unconscionable in the prevailing social environment in our society. Detractors point to the accumulation of huge student loans by the time of a student's graduation into a tight job market. But the fact is that over a life time, college education brings in a better economic outlook and a proper placement on the social hierarchy of needs. The temporary or short-term economic depression of a difficult job market is just one aspect in the dimensions of assessing post-education opportunities. One approach that can alleviate the economic concerns is to get the education objectives achieved in the most efficient, expedient, and expeditious manners. This will ensure that the student gets the most out of the education process as quickly as possible. Dilly-dallying with education will only lead to higher eventual costs and a decreased potential for making ends meet later on. An overall justification for education should be based on a mapping to the hierarchy of needs of individuals.

Educational Motivators

Motivation can involve the characteristics of the education process itself. In the theory of motivation, there are two motivational factors classified as the hygiene factors and motivators. Hygiene factors are necessary but not sufficient conditions for a contented individual. The negative aspects of the factors may lead to a disgruntled person, whereas their positive aspects do not necessarily enhance the satisfaction of the person. Examples include:

Educational policies: Bad policies can lead to the discontent of individuals while good policies are viewed as routine with no specific contribution to improving satisfaction.

Academic supervisor: A bad supervisor can make a person unhappy and less productive while a good supervisor cannot necessarily improve person's performance.

Working condition: Bad working conditions can impede students, but good conditions do not automatically generate improved productivity.

Study environment: A bad study environment can adversely affect student performance, but a good study environment does not, by default, improve student performance. There must be an external stimulus or driver for the student's higher performance.

Income: Low income can make a person unhappy, disruptive, and uncooperative, but an increase in income will not necessarily induce him or her to perform better. While a raise in salary will not necessarily increase professionalism, a reduction in salary will most certainly have an adverse effect on morale.

Social life: A miserable social life can adversely affect academic performance, but a happy social life does not imply better academic performance.

Interpersonal relationships: Good peer, superior, and subordinate relationships are important to keep a person happy and productive, but extraordinarily good relationships do not guarantee that he or she would be more productive.

Social and professional status: A low status can make a person to devolve to performing at his or her "level" whereas a higher status does not imply that he or she will perform at a higher level.

Security: A safe environment may not motivate a person to perform better, but an unsafe condition will certainly impede productivity.

Motivators are motivating agents that should be inherent in the work or study environment. If necessary, work should be redesigned to include inherent motivating factors. Some guidelines for incorporating motivators into jobs are presented below:

Achievement: The academic study process should incorporate opportunities for achievement and avenues to set personal goals to excel.

Recognition: The mechanism for recognizing superior performance should be incorporated into the study process. Opportunities for recognition should be built into the overall academic process.

Curriculum content: The curriculum work content should be interesting enough to motivate and stimulate the creativity of the individual. The amount of work and the organization of the work should be designed to fit the student's needs.

Responsibility: An individual should have some measure of responsibility for how his or her goals are pursued. Personal responsibility leads to accountability, which yields better performance. In this respect, a student should take responsibility for his or her academic performance.

Professional growth: The curriculum work should offer an opportunity for advancement so that the individual can set his or her own achievement level for professional growth within a reasonable plan of study.

The above examples may be described as study or work enrichment approaches with the basic philosophy that work or study can be made more interesting in order to induce an individual to perform at a higher level.

Establishing Educational Goals and Objectives

Students, with the assistance of parents, need to avoid goal conflict and inconsistency in educational plans. An educational goal consists of a detailed description of the overall pursuit and expectations from an academic pursuit. A goal is the composite effect of a series of objectives. Each objective should be defined with respect to its implication on the career goal of the student. A goal analysis helps to determine the courses of action with respect to what courses to take, what major to choose, and what project options to explore.

A goal-clarification approach should be used to set educational goals and objectives. This approach focuses on identifying specific goals and objectives that will assure success. Implementing the objectives, tracking performance over time, and providing ongoing assessment of strengths and weaknesses can help students set and enhance their goals. Business techniques such as "management by objectives" and "value stream mapping" can be used during the education planning process.

Adequate training is essential because it prepares students to do their jobs well by building the right knowledge that permits logical actions and decision making. If the right skills are provided for students, they can develop efficient work habits and positive attitudes that promote cooperation and teamwork for academic study and career paths. Some approaches to training as a complement to strict academic study are described below:

- Formal education in an academic institution
- On-the-job training through hands-on practice
- Continuing education short courses
- Training videos
- Group training seminars
- Role playing games

Some important aspects of setting educational goals and objectives include the following:

- Appraise existing categories and levels of technical skills.
- Consider the skills that would be needed in the future.
- Consider the possible career options.
- Appreciate the prevailing global workplace.
- Assess a combination of domestic and study-abroad opportunities.
- Leverage the infrastructure of existing technical training centers.
- Screen, select, and map skills, aptitude, and interests to training opportunities.
- Monitor progress and modify training process as needed.

- Synchronize the inflow and outflow of trainees with job potentials and national needs.
- Place trained manpower in relevant job functions.
- Leverage the working experience of professionals to guide education and training programs.
- Use documentations of results as inputs for planning future training programs.

Knowledge-Driven versus Income-Driven Education

The pursuit of education may be driven by the need for knowledge or the need for future income potential. In each case, the education objectives must be compatible with the characteristics and intrinsic attributes of the individual. Many changes are now occurring in academic programs in preparation for the future work place, which has become a benchmark for many strategic planners.

Are we all ready for the future work environment?

Is the present education process aligned with the future needs?

As the business world prepares to meet the technological challenges of the future, there is a need to focus on the people who will take it there. People will be the most important component of the "man-machine-material" systems that will compete in the future work place. Graduate and undergraduate educators should play a crucial role in preparing the work force for the future through their roles as change initiators and facilitators. Improvements are needed in undergraduate education to facilitate a solid graduate education.

Undergraduate education is the foundation for professional practice. Undergraduate programs are the basis for entry into graduate schools and other professional fields. To facilitate this transition, curriculum and process improvements are needed in education strategies. Educators, employers, and practitioners advocate better integration of Science, Technology, Engineering, and Mathematics (STEM) with the concepts of design and practice throughout university education. Such integration should be a key component of any education reform. Hurried attempts to improve education are being made in many areas. We now have terms like "Total Quality Management for Academia", "Just-in-Time Education," "Outcome-Based Education," and "Continuous Education Improvement." Unfortunately, many of these represent mere rhetoric that is not backed by practical implementation strategies or a funding base.

Enhancing STEM Education

Incorporating quality concepts into education is a goal that should be pursued at national, state, local, and institutional levels. Existing business models of quality management and continuous improvement can be adopted for curriculum improvement. However, because of the unique nature of academia, a re-definition of the business approaches will be necessary, so that the techniques will be compatible with the academic process. The basic concepts of improving product quality are applicable to improving any education process. A careful review of STEM curricula will reveal potential areas for improvement. This will help avoid stale curricula that may not adequately meet current and future needs of the society. For example, the basic scope of STEM education should be expanded to incorporate and embrace liberal arts and other social science areas that are very vital for the advancement of the society as a whole. This author has seen recent efforts by some schools to expand the STEM programs to STEMMA (Science, Technology, Engineering, Medicine, and Arts). This is a more robust approach to improving the education process.

The following specific symptoms of educational challenges have been noted:

- Increasing undergraduate attrition despite falling academic standards at many schools
- Decreasing teaching loads in favor of increasing dedication to research in higher education

- Migration of full professors from undergraduate teaching in favor of graduate teaching, sponsored research, and research center administration
- Watered down contents of undergraduate courses in the attempt to achieve retention goals
- Decreasing relevance of undergraduate courses to real-world practice
- Decreasing communication skills of college graduates
  Language is the expression of our thoughts in words. Grammar is the science of languages, and the art of speaking and writing correctly. If communication skills degrade, the expression of thought could be faulty.

Ethics in Education

Professional morality and responsibility should be introduced early to college students. Lessons on ethics should be incorporated into curriculum improvement approaches. Students should have a basic understanding of ethics and should appreciate the following requirements:

- Use knowledge and skill for the enhancement of human welfare.
- Be honest, loyal, and impartial in serving the public, employers, and colleagues.
- Strive to increase the competence and prestige of the chosen profession.
- Support and participate in the activities of professional and technical societies.

Life-long Learning

Education should not just be a matter of taking courses, getting good grades, and moving on. Life-long lessons should be a basic component of every education process. These lessons can only be achieved through a systems view of education. The politics of practice should be explained to students so that they are not shocked and frustrated when they go from the classroom to the boardroom.

Universities face a variety of real-world multi-disciplinary problems that are often similar to business operations problems. These problems could be used as test cases for solution approaches. Interdisciplinary student teams should be formed to develop effective solutions to societal problems. The author summarizes his view as shown below:

There is never one perfect solution;
There is never one single solution;
Only an integrated systems-focused solution can get us to our goals of solving societal problems.

Schools should increase their interactions with local businesses and industry, when available and possible. This will facilitate more realistic and relevant joint projects for students and working professionals.

The versatility of university education can be enhanced by encouraging students to take more cross-disciplinary courses to facilitate the interplay of STEM areas and liberal arts. Students must keep in mind that computer is just a tool and not the solution. For example, a word processor is a clerical tool that cannot compose a report by itself without the creative thinking and writing ability of the user. Likewise, a spreadsheet program is an analytical tool that cannot perform accurate calculations without accurate inputs from the user. Undergraduate and graduate education should be seen as contiguous components in the overall hierarchy of education process.

Chapter 2

Badiru's Equation of Success

Badiru's Equation of Student Success

Success, in any form, is a function of three factors governed by the mathematical expression below:

$$S = f(x, y, z)$$

where:

$x = Intelligence:$ Intelligence is an innate attribute, which every one of us is endowed with.

$y = Common\ Sense:$ Common sense is an acquired trait, which we learn from our everyday social interactions.

$z = Self\text{-}Discipline:$ Self-discipline is an inner drive (personal control), which helps to make the right decision in every situation.

With this equation, success is within our control. We cannot succeed on intelligence alone. We must apply common sense and self-discipline in order to achieve success.

© Adedeji Badiru, 1994

"I never dreamed about success. I worked for it."
     −   Esteel Lauder

Y ou may have the highest intelligence quotient (IQ) in the world, but if common sense and self-discipline are not used as the platform of application, the intelligence may be all for naught.

The equation of success expresses success as a function of intelligence, common sense, and self-discipline. Intelligence is the ability to acquire and apply knowledge while common sense refers to an individual's innate ability to use good judgment. Self-discipline represents a person's internal self control under external stimuli or influence. Meanwhile, success defines the attainment of a goal. A goal can relate to a personal quest, career objective, professional strive, social struggle, academic pursuit, or other desired end results. In each case, the goal can only be achieved through a judicious application of common sense coupled with a liberal demonstration of self-discipline. Although not an actual analytical model, the plot below conjectures how success can increase with increasing application of common sense and self-discipline.

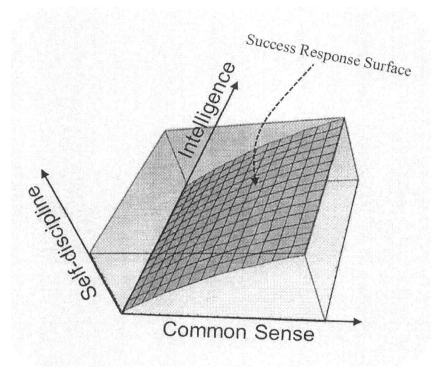

The relationship surface is, obviously, not smooth as shown in the hypothetical plot; but it gets the point across. If a social scientist were to actually conduct a human experiment, using a technique such as factor analysis, the surface may look as shown below. The right end of the plot indicates that success levels out somewhat at some point. Which is logical since success cannot increase indefinitely and there is a limit to both common sense and self-discipline. But for most of the operating ranges of human activities, the increasing profile of success does hold true with respect to increasing levels of common sense and self-discipline. Even then, dips and valleys can be expected in the profile of the plot as circumstances vary over the course of a person's pursuit of success.

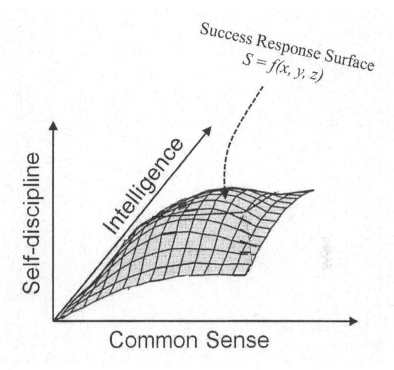

Fortunately, humans are endowed with sufficient basic intelligence to be successful at a variety of endeavors. Granted that there are varying levels of intelligence and capabilities, each student can still succeed at his or her own level of capabilities. But, within the boundary of the capabilities, a student must apply common sense and self-discipline in order to leverage and actualize the innate capabilities.

Consider the case of applying the above concept to New Year's resolutions. Self-discipline is the first step of accomplishing New Year's resolutions. This is the time of year when people make and break new-year resolutions. Some go through it just for fun. Some do it because it is a tradition. Yet, many do it with all seriousness. They often fail just the same. Why? It is often because innate self-discipline is lacking in our modern culture. People must develop and practice self-discipline in advance, well before the resolution season arrives. Otherwise, making resolutions will be all for naught again, as it has been in seasons past. Self-discipline is essential not only for achieving New Year's resolutions, but also for accomplishing all other goals throughout the year.

A popular quote says "Common sense is not so common." - Voltaire

This is what differentiates one person from another. What is not common is how different people apply the common sense. Explicit efforts must be directed at using the common sense, however rare it might be.

Along the same line, Rene Descartes' quote says:

"Common sense is the most widely shared commodity in the world, for every man is convinced that he is well supplied with it." - René Descartes

Yes, while we may all believe that we have the requisite common sense, we still must explicitly demonstrate that we can apply it. The application does not happen by default. Common sense relates to a situational awareness of how things are in the operating environment and how things should be in the pursuit of goals within that operating environment.

Common sense is not necessarily age dependent. Each age group demonstrates good common sense judgment accordingly to personal capabilities befitting of that age group. This recalls the common saying that goes as follow:

"Be wise with speed. A fool at forty is a fool indeed."
    – Edward Young English poet (1683 - 1765)

The above quote has inspired various uses of the adapted quote of:

"A fool at 40 is a fool forever,"

which suggests that a person without common sense in adulthood may never display this common-yet-uncommon personal characteristic.

Chapter 3
Intelligence

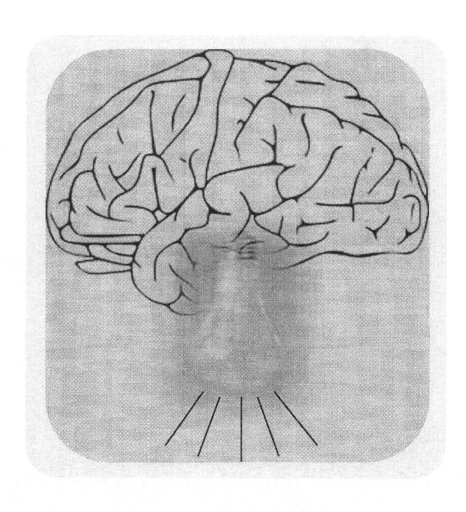

M easured quantitatively by IQ (Intelligence Quotient), natural intelligence is what makes a person self-aware and adaptive to the ambient stimuli. Even the highest level of intelligence does not guarantee success unless it is applied on a bed rock of common sense and self-discipline.

Initiating Success

Achieving success with getting things done is actually simple, if one initiates success right from the beginning. All it takes are a few key ground rules and perseverance, such as those listed below:

- Exercising commitment
- Exhibiting fortitude
- Extending compromise
- Demonstrating selectivity is what is done
- Embracing delegation when appropriate
- Displaying diligence
- Showing perseverance
- Teaming and partnering through:
  - Communication
  - Cooperation
  - Coordination
- Using the right tools
- Timing of what is done
- Outsourcing what is better done elsewhere

Maximize the utilization of each available hour of each day. Do, during the day, what you need daylight or working hours to do. Conversely, do not do, during the day, what you don't need daylight or working hours to do. In other words, use daylight hours appropriately to perform tasks that truly need daylight hours and put off until after-hours, those things that can be done at off hours.

Outsource tasks for which you have no skills, tools, or time; or from which you do not derive enjoyment or gratification. But you must retain control of accountability for the tasks.

Getting the Right Help

In order to do certain types of projects right, you must get the right person to do it. Don't over-indulge in DIY (Do-It-Yourself) mentality on all things. Some things are better done by those who know what they are doing; and those who have the right tools.

Even good projects can go bad for several reasons including the following:

- Ineffective management of requirements
- Inadequate risk appreciation and management
- Improper scope management
- Lack of full commitment
- Lack of streamlining
- Unrealistic expectations
- Action bluffing with no real action (see explanation below)

Managing Priorities

"The urgent problems are seldom the important ones."
 – President Dwight D. Eisenhower

When multi-tasking, we must evaluate what should have priority. An assessment of what is important versus what is urgent will help identify priority items. Not all tasks can be of equal "high" priority. What is important is not necessarily urgent; and what we often perceive as urgent is not really important. Tasks that are important and urgent have high priority. Those with low urgency and low importance fall in the "ignore" region; and do not deserve much attention in the overall scheme of things. Unfortunately, our lives are often ruled by urgency. With proper project management techniques, we can manage priorities by trading-off between what is urgent and what is important.

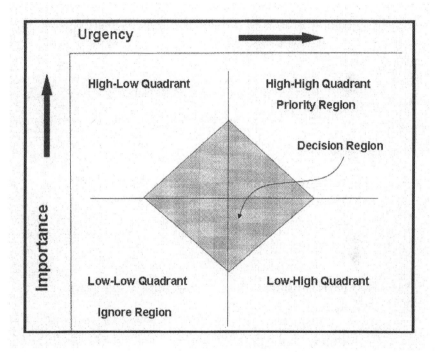

Using Personal Care

Many little choices that we make about what we do or don't do ultimately affect execution of projects. Make healthy personal choices; and you remain healthy to execute your projects successfully. Make personal bad choices, and they will come back to haunt you. Poor health and sour outlook impede the ability to execute projects efficiently.

Take Care of yourself so that you can take care of your tasks. Likewise, take care of your means of transportation. Take care of your car so that you can get to where you need to be promptly to do what you need to do in a timely manner. Many of our projects these days depend on accessible modes of transportation. Thus, project implementation can be very car-dependent. Getting to work on time, arriving on time for appointments, reaching a destination safe all can be impacted by the operational condition of our vehicles. For example, if we get our vehicles ready for harsh winter conditions, we will experience fewer car-related project delays. Winter transportation problems can be preempted by getting our cars ready for winter by doing the following:

- Service and maintain radiator system
- Replace windshield-wiper fluid with appropriate winter mixture
- Check tire pressure regularly
- Invest in replacing worn tires
- Maintain full tank of fuel during winter months to keep ice from forming in the tank and fuel lines
- Have ice scrapers accessible within passenger space in the vehicle; not stored in the trunk

Practicing Self Regulation

Have you ever considered yourself as a resource for your projects? That is, a resource that should be managed and regulated? Taking care of oneself is a direct example of human resource management, which is crucial for project success. Proper diet, exercise, and sleep are essential for mental alertness and positively impact the ability to get things done. Sleep, for example, affects many aspects of mental and physical activities. Sleep more and you will be amazed that you can get more done. This is because being well rested translates to fewer errors and preempts the need for rejects and rework. The notion that you have to stay up to get more done is not necessarily always true. Likewise, keep fit and get more done. Studies have confirmed that fit kids get better grades in school. Similarly, physically fit adults have been found to advance more professionally.

Avoiding Action Bluffing

It is imperative to avoid "management by bluffing." It is not always easy to accomplish what you "bluff" to do. Thus, cutting down on "action bluffing" and being selective with pledges will help streamline the list of things to do. Like an old IBM commercial said, "Stop talking. Start doing." This statement suggests the need to move on to the implementation stage of what needs to be done. Plans formulated so beautifully on paper or articulated in words mean nothing if they cannot be implemented.

In addition to overall strategies for getting to where we want to be, there must be tactical actions for getting there. This, essentially, is the purpose of project management. Project management is about creating the building blocks, called Work Breakdown Structure (WBS), that serve as steps toward the eventual project goal. Each element of the WBS represents something that must be done. Project management helps in getting those things done. That means we get things done through project management. WBS facilitates breaking a project up into manageable chunks. Project partition or segmentation improves overall project control at the operational level.

It is a fact that success can only be assured through dealing with manageable sets of tasks and activities. Whenever possible, consolidate activities. If we attempt to tackle multi-dimensional solutions that will require many players and participants, it would be more difficult to get everything to come together.

Developing a Strategy

Strategy is the vehicle for closing the gap between the current state and a desired future state. In order to build an effective strategy, we must have a honest assessment of the current state and a realistic evaluation of what can be achieved from that current state. For example, if current annual income is $75,000.00 and it is desirable to move up to $85,000.00, a strategy must be developed to close that gap. It is obvious that the strategy to be developed will be a function of the two end-points. If the disjoint between the two end points cannot be resolved, no amount of strategizing can close the inherent gap. Once a strategy has been formulated, the techniques of project management will be needed to actually implement the strategy. Thus, Strategy Building and Project Management are intimately tied together. They jointly produce desired results.

Project management is the vehicle of strategy. You cannot have a strategy without project management. Likewise, you cannot have project management without it being tied to a strategy. In the corporate world, much is made of the process of business strategy development; without a concerted effort toward project management. No wonder many corporate strategies fail.

In between strategy and project management lie risks. Every endeavor is subject to risks. If there were no risks, there would be no actions. Risks create opportunities. We must appreciate the risks that our projects portend and develop appropriate strategies to mitigate the risks. We must learn to strategize, streamline, and integrate project activities.

Time-Cost-Quality Tradeoffs

Always weigh cost versus time, cost versus quality, and time versus quality. Preempt problems by using multi-dimensional decision analysis. A simple example is a trade-off decision analysis of traveling by air or by road. The objective here is to get the travel done subject to the nuances of cost, time, and quality; which form the so-called concept of the "Iron Triangle," also known as "Triple Constraints," which examines the trade-offs between cost, time, and quality or budget, schedule, and performance. The cliché in this respect is "cost,

30

time, quality; which two do you want?" This implies that all three cannot be satisfied at equal levels. So, a trade-off or compromise must be exercised.

Case Example of Problem Preemption

Haste makes waste and rush makes crash. In over 37 years of driving on local, rural, back-road, and interstate roadways all over the USA, this author has never been involved in any type of accident (knock on wood); not even fender-benders. He has defensive and avoidance driving habits to avert being involved in accidents. Simple practices such as not following too close, not over-speeding, and being courteous to other drivers can significantly increase the chances of not being involved in an accident. It "takes two to tangle," and if one partner is unwilling and uncooperative in the tangling act, road collisions can be minimized. The last time this author was pulled over for traffic offense was in 1982 on Interstate 75 somewhere in Georgia, doing 71 where 55 was the limit. He still believes the stoppage was unjustified and was instigated by the fact that he was driving his beloved "hot rod" aka 1976 Chevy Camaro Rally Sport. He was pulled over from a long stretch of vehicles moving about the same speed. In other words, he was going with the traffic flow. He vowed since then never to allow himself to be subjected to any other unjustified traffic pull-over. He has respected and honored that vow ever since as a show of **self-discipline**. He refers to his conservative driving habits as simply "respecting yourself" so that others (especially the cops) can respect your space and time.

A couple of hours spent attending to being stopped by a state trooper or sorting out accidents details are hours taken away from some other projects. Over the years, this author has been asked how he manages to get so many things done so effortlessly. His usual response is "project management and problem preemption" This simply means using problem preemption techniques to avoid distractions that impede desired projects. Problem avoidance makes it possible to devote time to and focus on activities that really matter for project execution purposes.

Playing by the Rule

Playing by the rule up front saves time later on to get things done. Circumventing rules to cut corners can only lead to distractions and the need for time-consuming amendment later on. Time and effort invested in complying with rules and conforming to requirements pays off in the long run. The author describes himself as being a "self-imposed compliant conformist." This is a strategy that works by preempting trouble spots that would otherwise require resolution time. There will sometimes be a need for more time-consuming prudence in dotting all i's and crossing all t's upfront before concluding a deal, whatever the "deal" might be. If the prudence is not exercised upfront, it may come back to cause time-consuming resolution attempts and delays later on.

Getting on with It

In the final analysis of getting things done intelligently, the basic approach is to get on with it. There is never a perfect time to get something done. Each opportunity comes with its own constraints. Each constraint may entail its own certain level of necessity. This may be a necessity that must be attended to; such that avoiding the constraints is not possible. If one waits for the perfect time, most things will never get done. We must be willing to compromise, accept trade-offs, and move on. So, study on without further delay.

Chapter 4

Common Sense

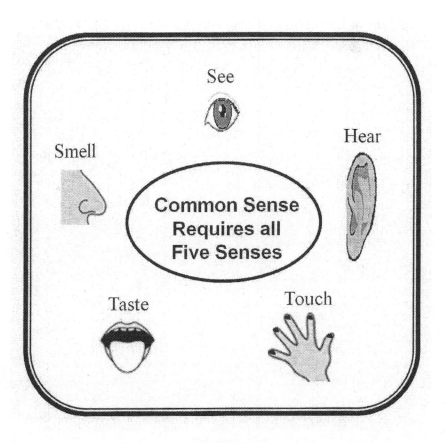

"The three great essentials to achieve anything worthwhile are, first, hard work; second, stick-to-itiveness; third, common sense."
  −   Thomas A. Edison

"Common sense is in spite of, not the result of, education."
  −   Victor Hugo

C ommon sense requires all five senses. To develop and apply common sense, a student must "feel" his or her environment as enumerated below:

- ➤ Look to see what is around you.
- ➤ Listen to hear the sounds of the environment.
- ➤ Touch to appreciate the texture of the surroundings.
- ➤ Smell the scents of the environment. "Smell the roses," so to speak.
- ➤ Taste to appreciate what is available to you.

Obviously, for each individual, the strength of one sense may be higher than the others. Nature has a way of making amendments, such that internal compensations take place to the extent that the overall capability of the individual may still be enhanced.

Managing Risks

As the saying goes, "you cannot accumulate if you don't speculate." Taking risk is part of getting things done. But the risk must be weighed against the prevailing cost and the opportunity to advance quality.

Balancing Study, Work, and Play

"Life is like riding a bicycle. In order to keep your balance, you must keep moving."
   − Albert Einstein

A student must balance personal engagements through study, work, and play. You must keep your feet properly planted on the tasks that matter and avoid falling over the edge of the steps of project management. In project management, one must deal with multiple objectives that often compete for time and resources. This is particularly critical when balancing regular work objectives with irregular personal objectives.

By using project management techniques, one set of objectives can be coordinated to support another set of objectives, and vice versa. A key requirement is to determine where and when compromises are possible and to what extent to exercise the compromises; particularly where work life versus home life is an issue.

Avoiding Haste and Waste

Take time to get things done right the first time. Haste makes waste and leads to non-value-adding corrective actions later on. You are your own best advocate. Humans have morbid fascination with other's failure, tragedy, and accidents. Don't allow your project to create a spectacle for rubber-necking onlookers.

Learning from Mistakes

"You must learn from the mistakes of others. You can't possibly live long enough to make them all yourself."
    −   Sam Levenson (1911 - 1980)

Mistakes are essential for learning and learning is essential for future project success. Plan what you need to do. Execute as planned. Learn from the project and document lessons learned. It is essential to close out a task. Closing a project is as important as initiating it. Not closing a task promptly often leads to project failure. Use the close-out to plan and initiate the next project. This process is summarized in the PELC (Plan-Execute-Learn-Close) quadrants of project success. While preparing for mistakes, we must also take precautions. As it is often said, **"measure twice and cut once."** Precautions that are taken to preempt errors result in saving time. Time, thus saved, can be redirected at more productive activities. Resources are scarce and we should not engage in wasteful mistakes.

Watching out for Time Robbers

Don't let unproductive activities "occupy" your time. These are activities that spread their "tentacles" throughout the span of a student's responsibilities. They become operational cancers that are difficult to eradicate. They can creep into every facet of your life without providing justification for their continuation and without any value-adding basis. If these time robbers are not avoided or terminated, they continue to consume time and resources while detracting from valuable accomplishments.

Getting more things done requires focusing on fewer things to do. Never spend time and effort on an activity that has little or no potential for providing value or generating a benefit. This implies that we must "separate the wheat from the chaff," when deciding on what needs to be done. We must be able to distinguish value-adding activities from wasteful activities. That means, we must operate "lean" and cut out non-value-adding activities. The Figure below is a Pareto Distribution showing that only about 20% of what we do is actually value-adding. As much as 80% of out activities could be going into wasteful engagements.

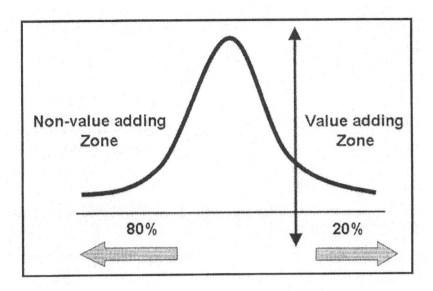

Attempting to do too much often leads to less being done. Tackling too much makes the "doer" more error prone, thereby leading to rework and subsequent waste of corrective time. The Pareto distribution is often extended to what is called ABC analysis, whereby items are organized into A, B, and C categories. These can be explained as follows:

A Category: Top 10% in order of value (absolutely essential).

B Category: Middle 80% in order of value (essential).

C Category: Bottom 10% in order of value (non-essential).

The C Category is often a "lost cause" and can be eliminated without much adverse consequence. By eliminating this, you will have more time to focus on the essential items. You will, consequently, be getting more done by focusing on fewer essential items. This leads us to the author's principle below:

Simplification helps to get more things done

Too often in life, we allow inconsequential lifestyles activities to rob us of time to get *really* valuable things done. You cannot hem-and-haw all day and then complain that you don't have enough time to get things done. Dilly-dally and shilly-shally ways of life rob us of opportunities to get the right things done promptly and satisfactorily. Below is the author's first principle of getting things done.

"To get more done, try and do less."

There are little nagging things that consume time every day. They are usually of little or no value. Eliminate them and you will have more discretionary time to yourself. Saving time through project management gives you time to do other things that you really want to do. If Albert Einstein had attempted to do several things in the years that he was fiddling with his theory of relativity, he probably would not have gotten it done when he did. Leonardo da Vinci (of the Mona Lisa fame) was reputed to not have been a good project manager because he died with several unfinished projects in various stages of incompleteness. What would have happened if he had focused on a few projects that were actually finished?

In order to get more done, you need to be more selective with social impositions. Such impositions create more things to do and less time to do the most crucial tasks. You don't have to visit Joe and Jane every time they issue an invitation for a gathering. You don't really have to attend every social function for which you have an invitation, no matter how sumptuous the Hors D'oeuvres might be. Identify what not to do at all. Identify what to do and in what order. Set goals and hold firm to the goals. Flip-flopping between setting goals and dismantling them with inaction does not leave room for actually getting things done.

Common Laws of Project Management

There are several guiding principles for project management. These are presented here as common laws of project management. They serve as philosophical and practical guidelines.

Parkinson's Law:

"Work expands to fill the available time."
Translation:- Idle time in project schedule creates opportunity for ineffective utilization of time.

Badiru's Theory:

"Grass always grows greener where you most need it to be dead."
Translation:- Problems fester naturally if left alone. Control must be exercised in order to preempt problems. Don't concede to others what you can control yourself.

Peter's Principle:

"People rise to the level of their incompetence."
Translation:- Get the right person into the right job.

Murphy's Law:

"Whatever can go wrong will."
Translation:- Project planning must make allowance for contingencies.

The Benefits of Starting Early

"Early to bed and early to rise makes a man healthy, wealthy, and wise."

    − Benjamin Franklin

Get started promptly with whatever needs to be done. What is worth doing is worth doing at the earliest opportunity. The old adage of "early to bed, early to rise" is very applicable to managing projects effectively and getting things done. The best things in life are done early in the morning. Milking cow is a good example. By contrast, most evils occur at night. The occurrence of crime is a good example. Farmers happily embrace the "early start" adage; and that is why this author loves farmers. The USA Army used to advertise that they "get more done before 9a.m. than most people get done all day." That is, indeed, the truth; and that is why this author loves the military. But the Army advertisement was phased out when it was realized that the young people of nowadays, who were being targeted as recruits, were not in favor of doing much early in the morning; if at all they get up that early. It is sad that the old adage of starting early has been replaced by the new truism of putting things off as late as possible. It is hoped that the lessons provided in this book will encourage readers to recapture the essence of what got our forefathers to the exalted level of work ethics that they handed down to us.

How to apply common sense:

- **Look around you and see what's going on around you, both good and bad.**

"Common sense is seeing things as they are; and doing things as they ought to be." - Harriet Beecher Stowe

Chapter 5

Self-Discipline

"Invest today in what will benefit you tomorrow."
    –   Deji Badiru

Discipline is the central topic of this book. Discipline is within your control. But it requires dedication, commitment, positive attitude, seriousness, and perseverance.

Success comes from self-discipline.

Self-discipline is a cornerstone of sustainable success.

Discipline is what helps you to get up in the morning to go to class when you'd rather continue to sleep.

Discipline is what helps you to overcome uninvited temptation.

Rita Mae Brown said,
"Lead me not into temptation; I can find the way myself."
   −   Rita Mae Brown, American writer, born 1944

Yes, refusing temptation is within your control.

Discipline helps you avoid over-drinking, over-eating, over-spending, and other undesirable indulgences.

Be mindful that "five minutes of temporary pleasure can lead to everlasting sorrow." Don't put the fun before the pain.

Exercising Self-Commitment

The single most important requirement for getting things done is self-commitment. It is through the discipline of self-commitment that projects, both large and small, can be executed successfully. Without self-commitment to do what needs to be done when it needs to be done, nothing can be accomplished satisfactorily. As a case in point, the number of those getting project management training and certification is increasing rapidly. Yet, the number of project failures, with significant cost, schedule, and performance implications, is also increasing. This is a fact that is inconsistent with theory and conventional expectation. If there is no self-commitment to execute a project according to plan, no amount of education, training, credentialing, tools, and techniques can rescue the project. Those who are most eloquent about what needs to be done, and how, are often the ones who falter when it comes to actually doing it. Each person must self-dedicate and self-actuate to make commitment to get things done the way they ought to be done.

Getting organized

Nothing demonstrates self-discipline more than being organized. There are all kinds of guides for getting organized. In the corporate environment, there are formal tools and techniques of pursuing a disciplined approach to work. In this chapter, the author prefers presenting the rigorous Japanese technique of 5s/6s. The belief is that these tools, applied on the small scale of personal needs, would be just as effective as they have been in the corporate work environment.

Work discipline through 5s and 6s

The "5s" and "6s" methodologies are Japanese techniques that demonstrate work place discipline through a series of words starting with the letter "s." When the first five words are used, we have "5s" and when six words are used, we have "6s." the words are as follow:

1. **Seiri (Sort):** This means distinguish between what is needed and not needed and remove the latter. The tools and materials in the workplace are sorted out. The unwanted tools and materials are placed in the tag area.

2. **Seiton (Stabilize):** This means to enforce a place for everything and everything in its place. The workplace is organized by labeling. The machines and tools are labeled with their names and all the sufficient data required. A sketch with exact scale of the work floor is drawn with grids. This helps in achieving a better flow of work and easy access of all tools and machines.

3. **Seison (Shine):** This means to clean up the workplace and look for ways to keep it clean. Periodic cleaning and maintenance of the workplace and machines are done. The wastes are placed in a separate area. The recyclable and other wastes are separately placed in separate containers. This makes it easy to know where every components are placed. The clean look of the work place helps in a better organization and increases flow.

4. **Seiketsu (Standardize):** This means to maintain and monitor adherence to the first three s's. This process helps to standardize work. The work of each person is clearly defined. The suitable person is chosen for a particular work. People in the workplace should know who is responsible for what. The scheduling is standardized. Time is maintained for every work that is to be done. A set of rules is created to maintain the first 3s's. This helps in improving efficiency of the workplace.

5. **Shitsuke (Sustain):** This means to follow the rules to keep the workplace 6s-right—"maintain the gain." Once the previous 4s's are implemented some rules are developed for sustaining the other S's .

6. **Safety:** This refers to eliminating hazards in the work environment. The sixth "s" is added so that focus could be directed at safety within all improvement efforts. This is particularly essential in high-risk and accident-prone environments. This sixth extension is often debated as a separate entity because safety should be implicit in everything we do. Besides, the Japanese word for Safety is "Anzen," which does not follow the "s" rhythm. Going

further out on a limp, some practitioners even include additional "s's". So, we could have 8s with the addition of Security and Satisfaction.

7. **Security** (e.g., job security, personal security, mitigation of risk, capital security, intellectual security, property security, information security, asset security, equity security, product brand security, etc.)

8. **Satisfaction** (e.g., employee satisfaction, morale, job satisfaction, sense of belonging, etc.)

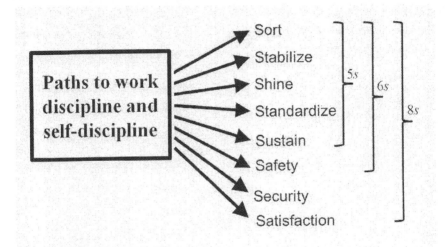

<u>**How to apply self-discipline**</u>:

• Think of the possible consequence of your actions.
• Don't let friends, leisure, and recreation "occupy" too much of your study time.

<u>**Discipline for Taking a Test:**</u> **Badiru's Four Read-Through Guide**

This author has guide for taking a test. It centers on reading a test question thoroughly before attempting to solve the test problem. Read a test question again and again before attempting to answer the question. The four read-through guide suggests reading a test question four times and it goes as follows:

- Read the test question for the first time, just for general orientation to the question.
- Read the question the second time, just to note and/or jot down the essential points or data.
- Read the question the third time. It is during this third time that you would start attempting to solve the problem. By this time, you would have seen the question "twice" before. This makes for a better understanding of the problem and all the requirements, givens, and unknowns.
- Read the question the fourth time. During this stage of reading, do a recapitulation of the problem, the boundary conditions, and a confirmation that you have answered the question as instructed.

One common example of the pitfall of not reading a question in its entirety is the famous 20-question test, in which the first instruction says to read every question before attempting to answer any of the 20 questions; and the last instruction says you don't have to answer any of the questions. Most students will impatiently start answering the questions as furiously fast as they can, because of the time constraint specified for the test. In the end, they never get to the end of the 20 questions within the limited time allotted for the test when, in fact, the test consists of only reading the 20 questions without having to do anything. Valuable time and stress are expended trying to beat the test time. This represents a big misapplication of effort and time. It takes a great amount of self-discipline to completely read a question before attempting to solve it. But if the upfront time is invested, it can save a lot of agony later on.

It is all about self-discipline.

Chapter 6

Recipe for an F

"Imagination is more important than knowledge."
    –   Albert Einstein

I magine it. Students have tried it. Badiru's recipe for an F is a reverse psychology approach to student encouragement. While composed to be comical, the recipe does get a student's attention …and it works.

The recipe is based on common excuses that students give in the attempt to get out of their academic responsibilities. Even though scores and scores of such excuses have been documented in the author's notes over the years, this particular recipe is limited to only ten of the classic examples. The recipe is displayed below in the usual handout format given to students at the beginning of each class. The recipe has worked well for entering freshmen, sophomores, juniors, and all the other classifications all the way through the doctoral level.

Show up for class: Big money is paid for every class in which you are enrolled. You take personal responsibility to attend all your classes, except in extenuating circumstances of illness, accident, family issues, financial reasons, and other unavoidable justifications.

Turn in assignments on time: The reason that a deadline is specified for an assignment is so that students can keep on track. Missing even one assignment creates a backlog, from which you may not be able to recover, at least not with a good grade.

Keep your work readable: A sloppy work will always earn a sloppy grade … always. By keeping your work clean, readable, and organized, you are making the instructor's job easier … and his/her life easier. For this, you are often rewarded with more lenient points. A clear and readable work ensures that the grader will be able to follow your logic and be able to determine where you deserve some credit and additional points, even if the final answer is erroneous.

Give no excuses: The outcome of your grade is your own responsibility, assuming that the instructor has done his or her own lecturing effectively. Presenting frivolous excuses amounts to attempting to shift your responsibility to the instructor. Many instructors take offense to this and will penalize you accordingly grade-wise when an opportunity arises.

Commit to your class time: Enrolling for a class represents a contract between the student and the university. If the university does it part in offering the class, it is your commitment to attend the class. If the class time does not fit your other "worldly responsibilities," then find other courses to enroll in or modify your personal schedule to fit the requirements of your educational commitments. As an undergraduate, putting outside work hours above school hours is like "putting the cart before the horse." Completing your college education will ensure more pleasurable work opportunities later on.

Equip yourself with what you need: Always ensure that you have what you need to get the job done promptly and effectiveness. Abraham Lincoln said:

"Give me six hours to chop down a tree and I will spend the first four sharpening the axe."

This quote points out the importance of getting your tool in the right working condition. It is your responsibility to have your own book, calculator, pen, pencil, paper, computer, etc. available and ready to serve you. You cannot succeed by going "a'borrowing" all the time. Occasion borrowing may be okay, but making a habit of it is inexcusable. Consider the following case example:

"A freshman bought a lifesaving tool, which is designed
to be kept in the car to cut through a seat belt if he
gets trapped. Well, he keeps it in the car trunk."

There is a place for everything and everything should be in its rightful place.

Consider every class meeting as most valuable: Indeed, every class meeting is valuable for realizing the eventual goal of the course. Otherwise, the class would be cancelled. To ask an instructor, "did I miss anything important?" is the most insulting query about the instructor's worth to the university. Of course, you will miss something important each time you miss a class meeting. The class will not wait for you and the instructor will not give you a private lecture, which will not be fair to the other students.

Take your responsibility as your own responsibility: No one else can be responsible for your class work. Accountability is very essential for student success. A simple thing like turning in your own assignment should be taken seriously. Barring being incapacitated and unable to turn in your work yourself, there is no reason to ask someone else to do it for you. If unavoidable circumstances dictate that you do this, then do not blame someone else when something goes wrong.

Class information should be received and used: Information related to class schedule, test times, and exam dates are often announced well in advance. Be sure you save and track all the important dates and times. The instructor is not your personal schedulers and reminder assistant.

If you've earned, you will get it: Grades are earned, not negotiated. There is no place for a grade of "incomplete" at the end of the term except in extreme cases such as illness. University policies and guidelines provide explicit information about when, where, and how an incomplete grade may be assigned. If you need to withdraw from a class in advance, do it within the specified grace period. Pushing the boundary of the instructor's mercy will only further solidify your assurance of failure, which is not the goal of being in the academic institution.

Chapter 7
Time Management

T ime is the basis for everything. Time, once lost, cannot be regained. The author's poem below presents his exhortation of the importance of time management.

"The Flight of Time

What is the speed and direction of Time?
Time flies; but it has no wings.
Time goes fast; but it has no speed.
Where has time gone? But it has no destination.
Time goes here and there; but it has no direction.
Time has no embodiment. It neither flies, walks, nor goes anywhere.
Yet, the passage of time is constant."
 –   © 2006 by Adedeji Badiru

Time is of the essence of managing your academic tasks. Task management can be viewed as a three-legged stool with the following three main components:

- Time availability
- Resource allocation
- Quality of performance

When one leg is shorter than the others or non-existent the stool cannot be used for its expected purpose. Time is a limited non-recyclable commodity, as evidenced by the opening poem. Industry leaders send employees to time management training sessions and continuously preach the importance of completing tasks on time. However, the one area where time management is most crucial is often overlooked and undervalued, personal task management. Task management, by definition, is in itself time management via milestone tracking of important accomplishments and bottleneck identification. There are only 24 hours in a day and one of the goals for a student is how to most efficiently use those 24 hours. The tendency is for students to sacrifice the time portion of the academic pursuit and still expect the same level of performance. This thought process is flawed and ultimately leads to failure. If an academic semester task that normally takes 12 weeks for completion is condensed into 4 weeks, this would represent a time compression of more than 60 percent. If we were to take the task management stool and reduce one of the legs by 60 percent, the stool would topple over. This is the same result, in terms of performance, when activity compression occurs. An analysis of time constraints should be a part of the student's feasibility assessment of his or her study responsibilities. Task planning, personal organization, and task scheduling all have a timing component.

Activity Precedence Relationships

The precedence relationships among tasks fall into three major categories of technical precedence, procedural precedence, and imposed precedence. Technical precedence requirements reflect the technical relationships among activities. For example, in conventional construction, walls must be erected before the roof can be installed. Procedural precedence requirements, however, are determined by policies and procedures that may be arbitrary or subjective and may have no concrete justification. Imposed precedence requirements can be classified as resource-imposed, project status-imposed, or environment-imposed. For example, resource shortages may require that one task be completed before another can begin, or the current status of a project (e.g., percent completion) may determine that one activity be performed before another, or the physical environment of a project, such as weather changes or the effects of concurrent projects, may determine the precedence relationships of the activities in the project.

An assessment of how tasks interrelate is a required element of not wasting time in task scheduling and management. Consider the quote below:

"It has been my observation that most people get ahead during the time that others waste." - Henry Ford

Chapter 8
Money Management

Money has value with respect to time. The time value of money is something that students are, typically, not conversant with. A dollar today is not the same as a dollar tomorrow. The same time value of money calculations that businesses and corporations use is what any ordinary consumer, for example, a student, would use to address money management challenges.

From a business perspective, capital, in the form of money, is one of the factors that sustain business projects or ventures in the enterprise of producing wealth. However, it is necessary to intelligently consider the implications of committing capital to a business over a period of time; the discipline of economic analysis helps us achieve that aim. The time value of money is an important factor in economic consideration of projects. This is particularly crucial for long-term projects that are subject to changes in several cost parameters. Both the timing and quantity of cash flow are important for personal money management. The evaluation of an alternative requires consideration of the initial investment, depreciation, taxes, inflation, economic life of the project, salvage value, and cash flow. Capital can be classified into two categories:

- Equity
- Debt

With the easy availability of credit cards for college students, more and more students are falling prey to the burden of debt. Apart from credit cards, educational student loans also create massive debt burdens that only get compounded over time.

Equity capital is owned by individuals and invested with the hope of making profit, whereas debt capital is borrowed from lenders such as banks. In this chapter, we explain the nature of capital, interest, and the fundamental concepts underlying the relationship between capital investments and the terms of those investments. These fundamental concepts play a central role in how an individual manages his or her money.

Nominal and Effective Interest Rates

The compound interest rate, which we will refer to as simply "interest rate," is used in economic analysis to account for the time value of money. Interest rates are usually expressed as a percentage, and the interest period (the time unit of the rate) is usually a year. However, interest rates can also be computed more than once a year. Compound interest rates can be quoted as *nominal interest rates* or as *effective interest rates*.

A *nominal interest rate* is the interest rate as quoted without considering the effect of any compounding. It is not the real interest rate used for economic analysis; however, it is usually the quoted interest rate because it is numerically smaller than the effective interest rate. It is equivalent to the annual percentage rate (APR), which is usually quoted for loan and credit-card purposes. The expression for calculating the nominal interest rate follows:

$$r = (\text{interest rate per period}) \times (\text{number of periods}).$$

The format for expressing r is as follows:

$r\%$ per time period t.

The effective interest rate can be expressed either per year or per compounding period. It is the effective interest rate per year that is used in engineering economic analysis calculations. It is the annual interest rate taking into consideration the effect of any compounding during

66

the year. It accounts for both the nominal rate and the compounding frequency. Effective interest rate *per year* is given by:

$$i = (1+i)^m - 1$$

When compounding occurs more frequently, the compounding period becomes shorter; hence, we have the phenomenon of continuous compounding. This situation can be seen in the stock markets.

Example

The nominal annual interest rate of an investment is 9%. What is the effective annual interest rate if the interest is payable, or compounded, quarterly?

Solution

Using the effective interest rate formula, the effective annual interest rate compounded quarterly is calculated as follows:

$$\left(1 + \frac{0.09}{4}\right)^4 - 1 = 9.31\%.$$

The slight difference between each of these values and the nominal interest rate of 9% becomes a big concern if the period of computation is in the double digits. The effective interest rate must always be used in all computations. Therefore, a correct identification of the nominal and effective interest rates is very important. See the following example.

Example

Identify the following interest rate statements as either nominal or effective:

    a. 14% per year
    b. 1% per month, compounded weekly

    c.   Effective 15% per year, compounded monthly

    d.   1.5% per month, compounded monthly

    e.   20% per year, compounded semiannually

Solution

    a.   This is an *effective interest rate*. This may also be written as 14% per year, compounded yearly.

    b.   This is a *nominal interest rate* since the rate of compounding is not equal to the rate of interest period.

    c.   This is an *effective interest for yearly rate.*

    d.   This is an *effective interest for monthly rate.* A new rate should be computed for yearly computations. This may also be written as 1.5% per month.

    e.   This is a *nominal interest rate* because the rate of compounding and the rate of interest period are not the same.

The basic reason for performing economic analysis is to provide information that helps in making choices between mutually exclusive projects competing for limited resources. The cost performance of each project will depend on the timing and levels of its expenditures. By using various techniques of computing cash flow equivalence, we can reduce competing project cash flows to a common basis for comparison. The common basis depends, however, on the prevailing interest rate. Two cash flows that are equivalent at a given interest rate are not equivalent at a different interest rate. The basic techniques for converting cash flows from an interest rate at one point in time to the interest rate at another are presented in this section.

Cash-flow conversion involves the transfer of project funds from one point in time to another. There are several factors used in the conversion of cash flows.

Let:

P=cash flow value at the present time period. This usually occurs at time 0.

F=Cash flow value at some time in the future.

A=series of equal, consecutive, and end-of-period cash flow. This is also called annuity.

t=a measure of time period. It can be stated in years, months, or days.

n=the total number of time periods, which can be in days, weeks, months, or years.

i=interest rate per time period expressed as a percentage.

In many cases, the interest rate used in performing economic analysis is set equal to the minimum attractive rate of return (MARR) of the decision maker. The MARR is also sometimes referred to as the *hurdle rate,* the *required internal rate of return (IRR),* the *return on investment (ROI),* or the *discount rate.* The value of the MARR is chosen with the objective of maximizing the economic performance of a project.

Compound Amount Factor

The procedure for the single payment compound amount factor finds a future sum of money, *F,* that is equivalent to a present sum of money, *P,* at a specified interest rate, *i,* after *n* periods. This is calculated as:

$$F = P(1 + i)^n$$

Example

A sum of $5,000 is deposited in a project account and is left there to earn interest for 15 years. If the interest rate per year is 12%, the compound amount after 15 years can be calculated as follows:

$$F = \$5,000(1 + 0.12)^{15} = \$27,367.85.$$

Present Worth Factor

The present worth factor computes P when F is given. The present worth factor is obtained by solving for P in the equation for the compound amount factor. That is,

$$P = F(1 + i)^{-n}$$

Suppose it is estimated that \$15,000 would be needed to complete the implementation of a project five years in the future, how much should be deposited in a special project fund now so that the fund would accrue to the required \$15,000 exactly in five years? If the special project fund pays interest at 9.2% per year, the required deposit would be:

$$P = \$15,000(1 + 0.092)^{-5} = \$9,660.03.$$

Uniform Series Present Worth Factor

The uniform series present worth factor is used to calculate the present worth equivalent, P, of a series of equal end-of-period amounts, A. The derivation of the formula uses the finite sum of the present values of the individual amounts in the uniform series cash flow, as shown below.

$$P = A \left[\frac{(1+i)^n - 1}{i(1+i)^n} \right]$$

Example

Suppose that the sum of \$12,000 must be withdrawn from an account to meet the annual operating expenses of a multi-year project. The project account pays interest at 7.5% per year compounded on an annual basis. If the project is expected to last ten years, how much must be deposited in the project account now so that the operating expenses of \$12,000 can be withdrawn at the end of every year for ten years? The project fund is expected to be depleted to zero by the end of the last year of the project. The first withdrawal will be made one year after the project account is opened, and no additional deposits will be made in the account during the project life cycle. The required deposit is calculated to be:

$$P = \$12,000 \left[\frac{(1+0.075)^{10} - 1}{0.075(1+0.075)^{10}} \right] = \$82,368.92$$

Uniform Series Capital Recovery Factor

The capital recovery formula is used to calculate the uniform series of equal end-of-period payments, A, that are equivalent to a given present amount, P. This is the converse of the uniform series present amount factor. The equation for the uniform series capital recovery factor is obtained by solving for A in the uniform series present amount factor. That is,

$$A = P \left[\frac{i(1+i)^n}{(1+i)^n - 1} \right].$$

Example

Suppose a piece of equipment needed to launch a project must be purchased at a cost of $50,000. The entire cost is to be financed at 13.5% per year and repaid on a monthly installment schedule over four years. It is desired to calculate what the monthly loan payments will be. It is assumed that the first loan payment will be made exactly one month after the equipment is financed. If the interest rate of 13.5% per year is compounded monthly, then the interest rate per month will be 13.5%/12 = 1.125% per month. The number of interest periods over which the loan will be repaid is 4(12) = 48 months. Consequently, the monthly loan payments are calculated to be:

$$A = \$50,000 \left[\frac{0.01125(1+0.01123)^{48}}{(1+0.01125)^{48} - 1} \right] = \$1353.82$$

Uniform Series Compound Amount Factor

The series compound amount factor is used to calculate a single future amount that is equivalent to a uniform series of equal end-of-period payments. Note that the future amount occurs at the same point in time as the last amount in the uniform series of payments. The factor is derived as shown below:

$$F = A\left[\frac{(1+i)^n - 1}{i}\right]$$

Example

If equal end-of-year deposits of $5,000 are made to a project fund paying 8% per year for ten years, how much can be expected to be available for withdrawal from the account for capital expenditure immediately after the last deposit is made?

$$F = \$5000\left[\frac{(1+0.08)^{10} - 1}{0.08}\right] = \$72,432.50$$

Uniform Series Sinking Fund Factor

The sinking fund factor is used to calculate the uniform series of equal end-of-period amounts, A, that are equivalent to a single future amount, F. This is the reverse of the uniform series compound amount factor. The formula for the sinking fund is obtained by solving for A in the formula for the uniform series compound amount factor. That is,

$$A = F\left[\frac{i}{(1+i)^n - 1}\right]_.$$

Example

How large are the end-of-year equal amounts that must be deposited into a project account so that a balance of $75,000 will be available for withdrawal immediately after the twelfth annual deposit is made? The initial balance in the account is zero at the beginning of the first year. The account pays 10% interest per year. Using the formula for the sinking fund factor, the required annual deposits are:

$$A = \$75,000 \left[\frac{0.10}{(1+0.10)^{12} - 1} \right] = \$3,507.25$$

Guide to money management

- Understand time value of money.
- Think like a business that needs to grow, thrive, and survive.
- Buy only what you can afford to pay for.
- Use credit card only for emergencies and unavoidable situations, such as car rental.
- Pay off credit cards at the earliest opportunity, of they will compound into a bigger debt.
- If you have an income, pay yourself first (as in savings) from your net income.
- Disposable income does not mean "dispose of it."
- Track your income.
- Track your spending.
- Modify your shopping habits.
- Avoid impulse buying.
- Conduct an inventory of what you already have, so that you don't duplicate purchases.
- Set a money accumulation goal and pursue it incrementally.

Chapter 9

Don't Quit

Success
You will see it when you believe it

Success is within your reach;
You'll see it when you believe it;
You'll believe it when you see it.
Believe in yourself;
Believe in your ability.
Exercise your dedication in the pursuit of success.
With self-belief, you will certainly see success.
So, don't ever quit; Never!

- Original composition by Adedeji Badiru, February 25, 2013

"Success isn't permanent, and failure isn't fatal."
    –   Mike Ditka

I f after doing your best in applying the equation of success, things still don't go well, please don't quit.

"There is no sunrise without sunset;
There is no life without death;
There is no success without failure."
        –   T. T. Rangarajan, Indian Guru

Success is often built on an experience of initial failure. When failure does happen, it should be not perceived as an absolute obstacle to success. A student must keep to the task of pursuing success not matter what the interim challenges might be.

Chapter 10
Inspirational Proverbs

"Don't judge each day by the harvest you reap but by the seeds that
you plant."
      –   Robert Louis Stevenson

B uilding life skills needed for success requires learning from direct experiences, observations, and inspirational social axioms. Below are some selected examples germane to the theme of this book. Many of the selections are the less common proverbs.

A bad beginning can make a good ending.
A student in debt is caught in a net.
A penny saved is a penny gained.
A stitch in time saves nine.
A wise man changes his mind sometimes; a fool never.
A word to the wise is enough.
Action speaks louder than words.
After a storm comes a calm.
All covet, all lose.
All bad things happen at night.
A pen is mightier than a sword.
All that glitters is not gold.
All work and no play makes Jack a dull boy.
All work and no fun makes Jane a dull gal.
All is well that ends well.
An empty bag will not stand upright.
An idle brain is the devil's workshop.
An ounce of discretion is worth a pound of wit.
An ounce of prevention is worth a pound of cure.
Appetite comes with eating.
Appetite for learning comes with reading.

As you make your bed, so you will lie on it.

As you sow, so you shall reap.

As you invest, so you shall collect.

Avoid evil and it will avoid you.

Be just before you are generous.

Be not the first to quarrel, nor the last to make it up.

Beggars cannot be choosers.

Better be alone than in bad company.

Books and friends should be few and good.

Brevity is the soul of wit.

By other's faults wise men correct their own.

By timely mending shall you save much spending.

Catch the bear before you sell his skin.

Catch who catch can.

Charity begins at home, but should not end there.

Cheapest can be dearest.

Curses are like chickens, they come home to roost.

Children are what you make of them.

Courtesy costs nothing.

Cut your coat according to your cloth.

Delays are dangerous.

Devil takes the hindmost.

Diligence is a great teacher.

Discretion is the better part of valor.

Distance lends enchantment to the view.

Do as you are told and you shall reap the reward.

Do not put all your eggs in one basket.

Do not count your chickens before they are hatched.

Do not spur a willing horse.

Early to bed, early to rise, makes a person healthy, wealthy, and wise.

Eat to live, but do not live to eat.

Employment brings enjoyment.

Empty vessels make the most noise.

Enough is better than too much.

Every cloud has a silver lining.

Every dog has his day.

Every little helps.

Every man must carry his own cross.

Every why has a wherefore.

Everyone can find fault, but few can do better.

Everyone thinks his own burden the heaviest.

Everything comes to those who wait.

Example is better than precept.

Experience teaches.

Extremes are dangerous.

Facts are stubborn.

Failure teaches success.

Fall not out with a friend for a trifle.

Fancy kills and fancy cures.

Fingers were made before forks.

Fire is a good servant, but a bad master.

Flattery brings friends, truth enemies.

Flies are easier caught with honey than with vinegar.

Follow the river and you will find the sea.

Fortune favors the brave.

Give and spend and God will send.

Good beginnings make good endings.

Good to begin well, better to end well.

Grass grows greener where you most need it dead.

Great haste makes great waste.

Great profits, great risks.

Great talkers are little doers.

Half a loaf is better than no bread at all.

Hasty climbers have sudden falls.

He knows most who speaks least.

He laughs best that laughs last.

He that comes first to the hill, may sit where he will.

He that goes a-borrowing, goes a –sorrowing.

He that knows nothing, doubts nothing.
He that will eat the kernel must crack the nut.
He who ceases to pray ceases to prosper.
He's no man who cannot say "No."
Home is home, though it never be homely.
Hope is the last thing that we lose.
If the cap fits, wear it.
If wishes were horses, beggars might ride.
If you wish for peace, prepare for war.
Ill got, ill spent.
In for a penny, in for a pound.
It is a long lane that has no turning.
It is always time to do good.
It is easier to get money that to keep it.
It is easier to pull down than to build.
It is never too late to mend.
It takes two to make a quarrel.
Jack of all trades and master of none.
Kind words are worth much, but cost little.
Kindle not a fire that you cannot put out.
Kindness begets kindness.
Least said, soonest mended.
Little strokes fell great oaks.
Live not to eat, but eat to live.
Loans and debts make worries and frets.
Lost time is never found.
Make hay while the sun shines.
Make short the miles, with talk and smiles.
Manners maketh man.
Many hands make light work.
Many straws may bind an elephant.
Marry in haste, repent at leisure.
Men make houses, women make homes.
Nearest is dearest.

Neither wise men nor fools can work without tools.

Never a rose without thorns.

Never cross the bridge before you come to it.

Never dam the bridge that you have crossed.

Never do things by halves.

Never look a gift horse in the mouth.

Never put off till tomorrow what may be done today.

Never too old to learn; never too late to turn.

Never trouble trouble till trouble troubles you.

New brooms sweep clean.

No gains without pains.

None so blind as those who will not see.

None so deaf as those who will not hear.

Nothing succeeds like success.

Oaks fall when reeds stand.

Of one ill come many.

Of two evils, choose the less.

Old birds are not caught with chaff.

On a long journey, even a straw is heavy.

One can live on little, but not on nothing.

One fool makes many.

One may sooner fall than rise.

One swallow does not make a summer.

One Today is worth two Tomorrows.

Other fish to fry.

Out of debt, out of danger.

Penny wise, pound foolish.

Practice thrift or else you'll drift.

Praise makes good men better and bad men worse.

Pride goes before a fall.

Procrastination is a thief of time.

Punctuality if the heart of success.

Punctuality if the soul of business.

Put not your trust in money; put your money in trust.

Put your own shoulder to the wheel.

Reckless youth makes rueful age.

Rumor is a great traveler.

Saying is one thing, doing is another.

Second thoughts are best.

Set not your loaf in till the oven is hot.

Show me a liar and I'll show you a thief.

Silence gives consent.

Six of one and half a dozen of the other.

Slow and steady wins the race.

Small beginnings make great endings.

Soft words break no bones.

Soft words win hard hearts.

Some men are wise and some are otherwise.

Sometimes the best gain is to lose.

Soon hot, soon cold.

Speak little but speak the truth.

Speak well of your friends, and of your enemy nothing.

Speaking without thinking is shooting without aim.

Speech is silver, silence is golden.

Spilled salt is never all gathered.

Still water runs deep.

That which is evil is soon learned.

That which proves too much proves nothing.

The best of friends must part.

The darkest hour is nearest the dawn.

The exception proves the rule.

The fountain is clearest at its source.

The game is not worth the candle.

The goat must browse where she is tied.

The heart sees farther than the head.

The less people think, the more they talk.

The morning sun never lasts the day.

The pot calls the kettle black.

The receiver is as bad as the thief.

The stone that lieth not in your way need not offend you.

The tongue always lashes the aching tooth.

The unexpected always happens.

The wise makes jests and the fool repeats them.

There are two sides to every question.

There could be no great ones if there were no little.

There is a "But" in everything.

There is no venom like that of the tongue.

There is a salve for every sore.

They who only seek for faults find nothing else.

Those who do nothing generally take to shouting.

Those who make the best use of their time have none to spare.

Time and tide wait for no man.

Time cures more than the doctor.

Time is the best counselor.

Tit for tat is fair play.

To err is human, to forgive is divine.

To forget a wrong is the best revenge.

To know the disease is half the cure.

To make one hole to stop another.

To make two bites at one cherry.

To scare a bird is not the best way to catch it.

Too many cooks spoil the broth.

Too much of one thing is good for nothing.

Train a tree when it is young.

Tread on a worm and it will turn.

True love never grows old.

Trust, but not too much.

Two eyes see more than one.

Two is company, three is none.

Two hungry squirrels never quarrel.

Two wrongs do not make a right.

Undertake no more than you can perform.

Uneasy lies the head that wears the crown.

Union is strength.

Vice is its own punishment, virtue its own reward.

Walls have ears.

Wash your dirty linen at home.

Waste makes want.

Waste not want not.

We can live without our friends, but not without our neighbors.

Well begun is half done.

What belongs to everyone belongs to nobody.

What can't be cured must be endured.

What cost nothing is worth nothing.

What is learned in the cradle lasts to the crypt.

What's done can't be undone.

What is worth doing at all is worth doing well.

What man has done, man can do.

What the eye does not admire, the heart does not desire.

What the eyes don't see, the heart does not grieve for.

What the heart thinketh, the tongue speaketh.

When a man is going downhill, everyone will give him a push.

When in Rome, do as the Romans do.

When money is taken, freedom is forsaken.

When poverty comes in at the door, love flies out of the window.

When the cat is away, mice will play.

When the wine is in, the wit is out.

When two friends have a common purse, one sings and the other weeps.

When wits meet, sparks fly out.

Where ignorance is bliss, it is folly to be wise.

Where there is nothing to lose, there is nothing to fear.

While the grass grows the horse starves.

Who chatters to you will charter of you.

Who gossips to you will gossip of you.

Who judges others is only condemning himself.

Who knows most says least.

Wilful waste makes woeful want.

Wine and wenches empty men's purses.

You cannot get blood out of a stone.

You cannot shoe a running horse.

You never know till you have tried.

Young men think old men fools; old men know young men to be so.

Youth and age will never agree.

Youth lives on hope, old age on remembrance.

Zeal without knowledge is a runaway horse.